BORN to Be WILD

Baby Animals and Their Parents

written by Jennifer Li Shotz

illustrated by Yogesh Mahajan

CARING CREATURES

A penguin dad carefully balances a large, smooth egg on top of his bumpy feet. He's not playing a game—it's his way of keeping his egg safe and warm until it hatches.

An alligator mom cracks open her massive jaw and bares her terrifying teeth. Is she about to attack? Nope. She's letting her baby climb inside her mouth to hide from danger.

Beaver parents chew through trees and carry heavy piles of sticks and logs. They use the wood to build a safe, cozy shelter for their little ones.

Not all types of animals take care of their babies. But the ones that do work hard at this important job, just like human parents.

And like human babies, young animals learn from their parents as they grow. One day, they will be able to survive on their own.

PARENTING THE PENGUIN WAY

Bone-chilling winds whip across fields of ice. There's no shelter in sight. This is Antarctica, the coldest, driest, windiest place on Earth. It's also home to emperor penguins. Raising a baby penguin, or chick, here is not easy. A mother and father penguin must both work hard to help their little one survive.

Egg Warmer

In May or June, an emperor penguin mom lays one egg about the size of a softball. This happens right before the coldest season in Antarctica.

Then, Mom leaves on a long journey to the ocean to hunt for fish. The father stays behind to take care of the egg. Dad keeps it safe on top of his feet and under his warm feathers . . . for up to seventy-five days!

How to be an Amazing Penguin Dad in 3 Easy Steps

1. Balance the egg on your feet. Keep it warm with your body.

2. Stand there for about two months. Don't let that egg touch the ice!

3. Don't leave to get food. If you're hungry, just be patient. You can eat in a few weeks when Mom gets back.

Dinnertime!

Chicks chirp to let their parents know when they are hungry. If a chick hatches before its mother comes back, the father feeds it with liquid he spits up. When Mom returns, she spits up fish she has eaten right into her chick's mouth. It's her turn to care for the little bird while Dad travels to the ocean to hunt.

COOL FACT

It's hard for people to reach the icy places where emperor penguins live. So scientists use pictures taken from space to find these birds and count them. They search the photos for penguin poop stains on the ice to help them find the birds.

Cozy Toes

A newly hatched chick stays on its parents' feet for a few weeks, until its feathers are thick enough to keep it warm. The chick snuggles under a flap of skin called a brood pouch.

One Huge, Happy Family

Emperor penguins live in groups called colonies. A colony can have more than 5,000 adults and chicks.

Birds in a colony help each other stay warm by huddling together. They take turns shuffling to the center of the huddle, where it's nice and toasty. Then they move to the outer edge of the group again, giving others a chance to warm up.

Buddy System

When chicks are big enough, their parents sometimes go hunting and leave the babies alone. The young birds huddle in groups to keep each other warm, just like their parents taught them.

COOL FACT

Emperor penguins dive deeper than any other bird. They can stay underwater for more than twenty minutes while they hunt for fish.

BIG PENGUIN, LITTLE CHICK

ADULT

Emperor penguins are the largest type of penguin. An adult is about as tall as a six-year-old child.

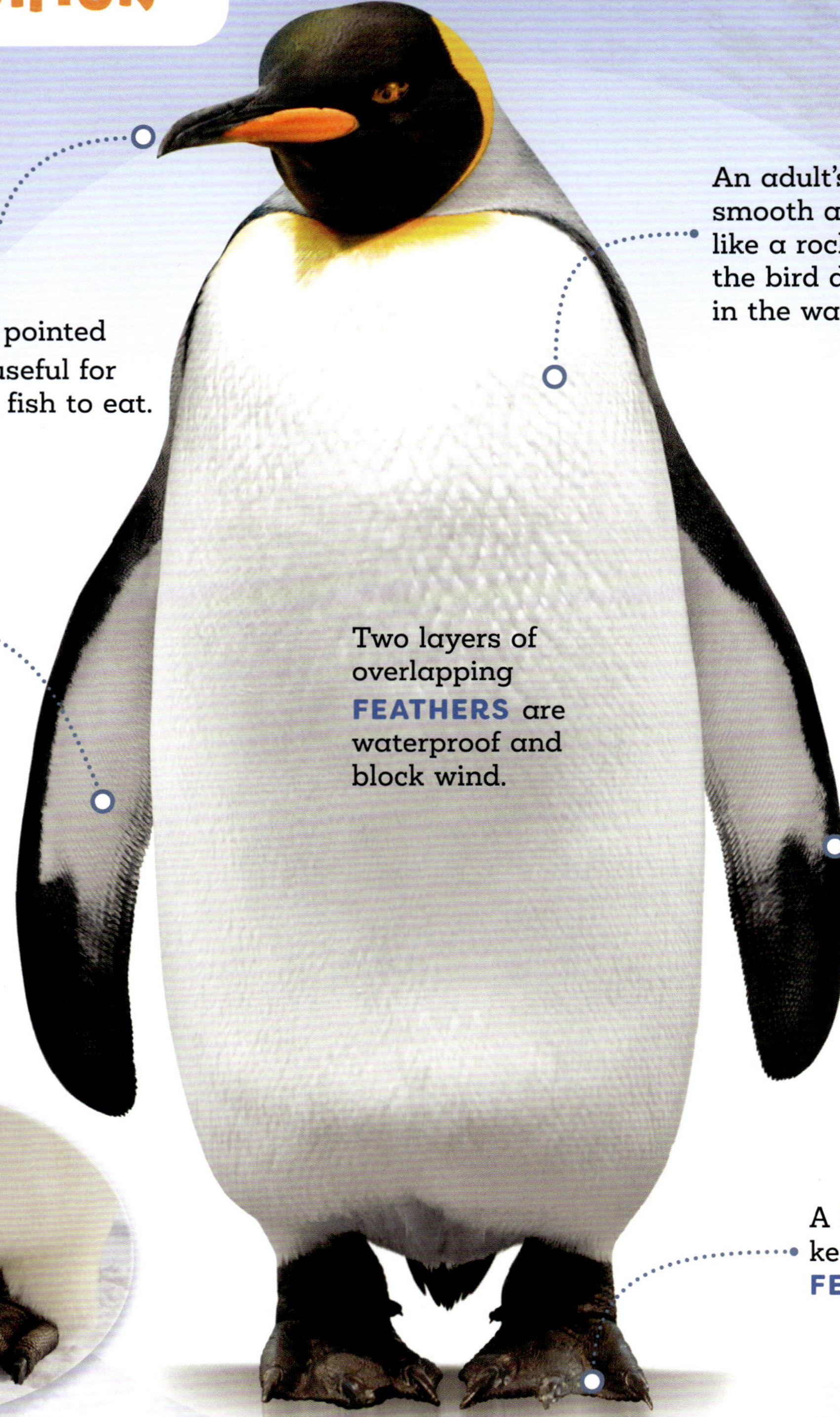

A sharp, pointed **BILL** is useful for catching fish to eat.

An adult's **BODY** is smooth and shaped like a rocket. This lets the bird dive and glide in the water.

Penguins can't fly, but they use their **WINGS** like flippers underwater.

An adult's **COLORS** help it blend in while swimming. Seen from above, its black back blends in with dark ocean water. Its white belly is hard to see from below.

Two layers of overlapping **FEATHERS** are waterproof and block wind.

Sharp **CLAWS** grip the ice. Emperor penguins can even climb steep ice cliffs!

A layer of fat keeps a penguin's **FEET** warm.

CHICK

When it hatches, an emperor penguin weighs about as much as an apple.

A chick's **BODY** isn't heavy enough for it to dive and swim underwater yet.

A chick's **COLORS** are different from those of an adult. It is light gray with a white-and-black face, and has no orange markings.

A chick's soft, downy **FEATHERS** don't offer much protection from the cold. They are not waterproof either. That's why chicks need help from their parents to stay warm.

An adult uses its **BROOD POUCH**, a flap of skin covered with feathers, to keep an egg or chick warm. Both males and females have brood pouches.

ADORING ALLIGATOR MOMS

A mother alligator uses her long snout, strong jaws, and sharp teeth to chomp down on a meal. But alligator moms also use their mouths to protect their young. Baby alligators are called hatchlings. A mother alligator opens her big mouth and lets hatchlings climb inside. Then she carefully carries them from place to place. Sometimes hatchlings stay inside Mom's mouth to keep away from danger. It's a safe hiding spot behind all those teeth!

Mom on Duty

Alligators live by rivers, swamps, and lakes in the southeastern United States. Females lay their eggs in nests. Then they cover the nests with grass and sticks to hide the eggs from hungry creatures. An alligator mom watches over her nest for about two months, until the babies hatch.

Hatchlings find a safe perch on top of their mother's back or head. Young gators often jump off into the water for a swim while their mom stays nearby to protect them. Then the babies climb back up and do it again.

GATOR GAB

Alligators constantly lose their teeth and grow new ones. During its lifetime, a gator grows as many as 3,000 teeth!

Hey, Mom!

Hatchlings make a chirping sound that alerts their mother about where they are. If danger is near, Mom hisses or swishes her tail around to scare other animals away.

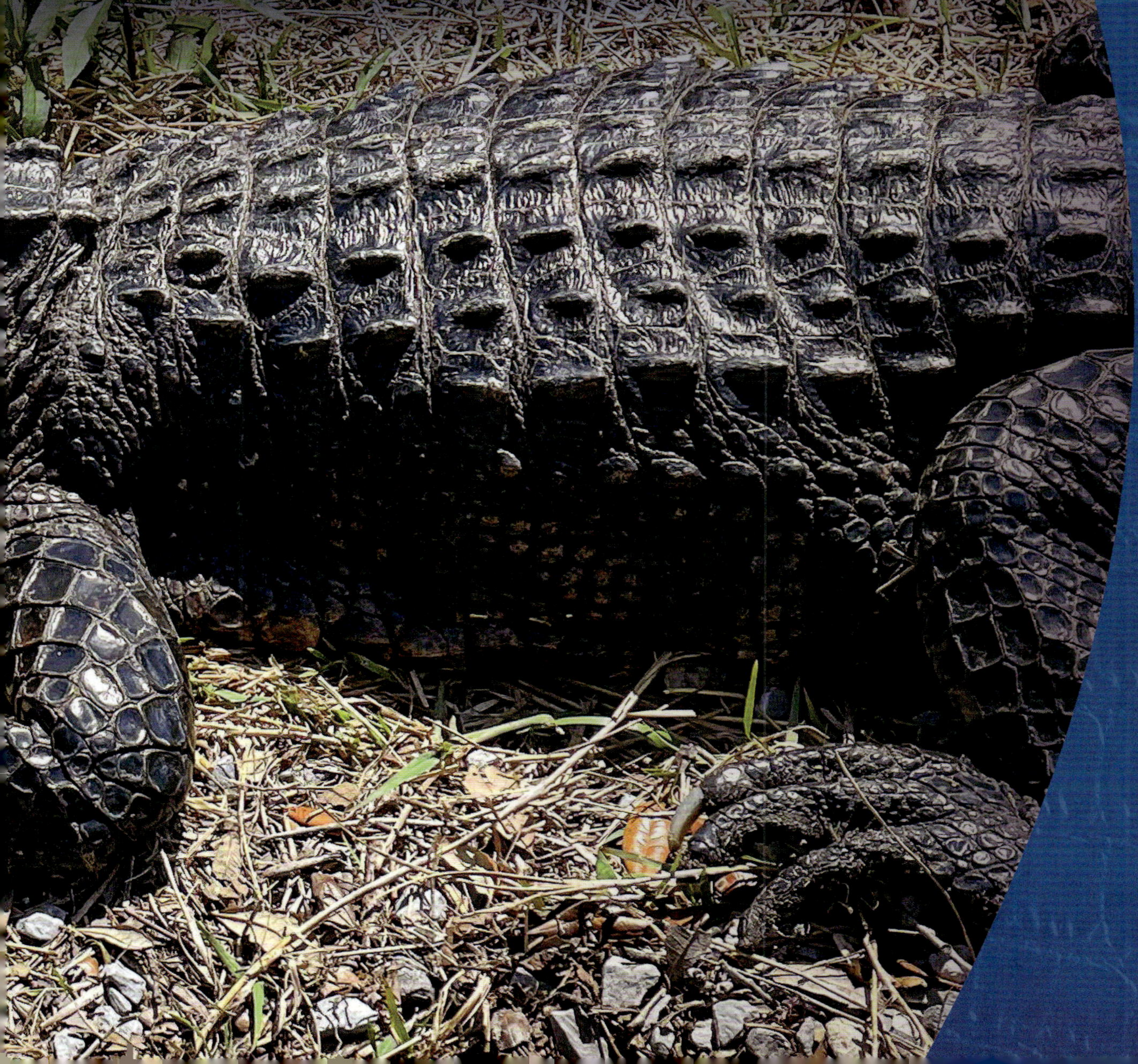

How to Hatch in 3 Easy Steps

1. Chirp to let Mom know you're ready to come out.

2. Use the special egg tooth on your snout to crack your shell.

3. Climb out of your shell and into Mom's mouth for a ride to the water.

Now, enjoy your first swim!

Hidden Hunters

A lurking alligator can be hard to spot. Its eyes, ears, and snout poke just above the surface while its terrifying teeth and claws stay hidden underwater. By blending in and staying perfectly still, alligators can surprise animals they want to eat, like fish, turtles, frogs, birds, and raccoons.

Practice Makes Perfect

An alligator mom does not teach her hatchlings how to hunt. Instead, she watches over her young ones as they figure it out on their own. Hatchlings start out by catching insects and small fish.

GATOR GAB

The word *alligator* comes from *el lagarto*, or "the lizard" in Spanish.

Alligators have been around for millions of years. They lived at the same time as dinosaurs!

BIG ALLIGATOR, LITTLE HATCHLING

ADULT

A male can be $4\frac{1}{2}$ meters (15 feet) long, the length of a car. Females are about $2\frac{1}{2}$ meters (8 feet) long.

A clear inner **EYELID** keeps out water but lets gators see while they swim.

Flaps of skin close off **EARS** and **NOSTRILS** underwater.

Thick, tough, scaly **SKIN** protects like a suit of armor. The color makes the gator hard to see in dark water.

An alligator's **JAW** crushes prey with one of the strongest bites of any animal.

Webbed hind **FEET** push through the water.

HATCHLING

When it hatches, a gator is about 20 centimeters (8 inches) long, a little longer than a hot dog bun.

A hatchling's **SKIN** has yellow stripes, which help it hide in the grasses near the nest.

Watch out! Gators are born with a mouth full of sharp **TEETH**.

A hatchling's **TAIL** helps it swim, but it's not yet strong enough to fight off large animals.

A large, powerful **TAIL** swishes from side to side for swimming. An alligator also uses its tail to defend itself.

BEAVER FAMILY FUN

Beaver families stick close together. Mom and Dad keep a careful eye on their babies, or kits. Parents protect kits from animals that want to eat them, like wolves and foxes.

Water World

Beavers make their homes in ponds, lakes, and rivers across the United States and Mexico. Kits tag along with their busy parents as they swim, search for food, and chew down trees.

BEAVER BITES

Kits often catch a ride . . .

on Mom's tail . . .

on her back . . .

and even in her mouth.

Alarm System

SPLASH! If a beaver senses danger, it loudly slaps its tail on the water. The noise alerts the kits that it's time to run and hide. It also scares off other animals that might hurt the kits.

BEAVER BITES

Beavers live with their parents until they are two years old.

Beaver teeth never stop growing. Chewing on trees helps grind down the teeth.

Busy Builders

Beavers are nature's construction crews! They chew through trees and shrubs. Then they carry the branches to a nearby river or stream. They pile up the wood to form a dam, which is like a wall across the river.

The dam blocks water from passing through. The water rises up, making a pond where beaver families can live. Animals like fish, frogs, birds, and insects live there too.

How to Build a Dam in 3 Easy Steps

1. Chew down trees with your long, sharp teeth.

Lodge Life

Beavers build homes called lodges in the safe ponds created by their dams. From the outside, a lodge looks like a pile of sticks. But inside is the den, an open area where the beaver family lives. A hole lets in fresh air for them to breathe. Kits are born in the warm, dry top part of the lodge.

To enter the lodge, beavers swim through a hole that's under the water. That makes it hard for animals that might harm kits to get inside.

BIG BEAVER, LITTLE KIT

ADULT

A fully grown beaver is about as big as a medium-sized dog.

Thick, oily **FUR** helps a beaver stay toasty warm and dry underwater.

NOSTRILS and **EARS** can close up to keep out water.

Strong, orange **TEETH** are shaped for cutting.

FRONT PAWS have five fingers to grab branches and food.

Webbed **BACK PAWS** help beavers swim.

KIT

At birth, a young beaver measures about 18 centimeters (7 inches) long, about the length of a banana.

Kits are born with a full coat of **FUR**.

Kits are born with their front **TEETH**, so they can get right to work chewing.

A wide, flat **TAIL** helps a beaver steer in the water and balance on land.

Like adults, kits have webbed toes on their **BACK PAWS**. But they can't dive underwater until they are about two months old.

BEAVER BITES

Thousands of years ago, giant beavers the size of bears lived in what is now North America.

BABY STEPS

It's a big world out there for baby penguins, alligators, and beavers. They must stay safe from other animals. They have to learn to find food, keep warm, and look after themselves. Luckily, they have their parents to watch out for them and teach them how to survive.

Animal parents have an important job raising their little ones. Many creatures use special body parts to keep babies safe. Emperor penguins use their feet and feathers. Alligators use their enormous mouths. Beavers use their teeth and tails.

With their parents' help, these baby animals chirp, waddle, and chew their way into adulthood.